チャコ専用

クロ
田代島

CATLAND

ねこランド

ALSO BY SARAH ARCHER

Midcentury Christmas
The Midcentury Kitchen

CATLAND

ねこランド

The Soft Power of Cat Culture in Japan

SARAH ARCHER

THE COUNTRYMAN PRESS

A division of W. W. Norton & Company

Independent Publishers Since 1923

For information about permission to reproduce selections from this book, write to Permissions, The Countryman Press, 500 Fifth Avenue, New York, NY 10110

For information about special discounts for bulk purchases, please contact W. W. Norton Special Sales at specialsales@wwnorton.com or 800-233-4830

Manufacturing by ToppanLeefung

Book design by Faceout Studio, Paul Nielsen

Production manager: Devon Zahn

Library of Congress Cataloging-in-Publication Data

Names: Archer, Sarah, author.
Title: Catland : the soft power of cat culture in Japan / Sarah Archer.
Description: New York, NY : The Countryman Press, [2020] | Includes
      bibliographical references and index.
Identifiers: LCCN 2019059883 | ISBN 9781682684733 (hardcover) |
      ISBN 9781682684740 (epub)
Subjects: LCSH: Cats—Japan—History. | Japan—Social life and customs.
Classification: LCC SF447 .A726 2020 | DDC 636.800952—dc23
LC record available at https://lccn.loc.gov/2019059883

The Countryman Press
www.countrymanpress.com

A division of W. W. Norton & Company, Inc.
500 Fifth Avenue, New York, NY 10110
www.wwnorton.com

10 9 8 7 6 5 4 3 2 1

For Mr. K, who brought me into the fold.

NOTED CAT LANDMARKS of JAPAN

SEKIKAWA VILLAGE CAT HUT SOCIETY

猫神社
(Cat shrine)

TAJIROSHIMA CAT ISLAND

MURASAKI-YU PUBLIC BATH

GOTANJOJI TEMPLE

JALALA CAT CAFÉ

ONOMICHI CITY MUSEUM OF ART

UMENOMIYA SHRINE

CAT BOOKSHOP

NYANNYANJI TEMPLE

GOTOKUJI TEMPLE

OKAWA KAGU FURNITURE

TOMIMOTO NINGYOU MANEKI NEKO FACTORY

Sendai

Tokyo

Kyoto

Hiroshima

Kochi

Fukuoka

CONTENTS

Cat priest Koyuki poses near Tanabe Castle, Maizuru, during cherry blossom season.

INTRODUCTION

序言

Imagine you're reading the news, and you come across an article about a new product or service that caters to cats. Maybe it strikes you as unusually thoughtful, or it looks exceptionally well-crafted. Perhaps it appears to have been undertaken with a seriousness of purpose and attention to detail that would rival that of any human-centered endeavor—and this seriousness, in and of itself, is irresistibly endearing. Do you have any doubt where this hypothetical cat product or service comes from? You do not: it's from Japan.

You know it, and so does Google: start typing "Why do the Japanese love . . ." or "Why does Japan love . . ." and you'll find that "cats" are invariably among the top one or two suggested search terms. Cats and cat imagery are woven into the fabric of daily life in Japan to an extraordinary degree. They have cat cafés, cat hotels, cat shrines, cat islands, cat-themed bookshops and stationery stores, a Hello Kitty theme park, and a famous cat tailor (that is, a person who makes clothes for cats, not the other way around). And in countless restaurants and shop windows throughout Japan, you'll find bright-eyed ceramic cat figurines with one paw raised, toe-side out, welcoming you inside. The *maneki neko*, or "beckoning cat," has been a fixture of the Japanese landscape since at least the turn of the 20th century.

An array of maneki neko figurines at the Baigetsu Tomimoto Doll Factory, Inc., in Tokonome.

C
A
T
L
A
N
D

But aren't there cats and "cat people" everywhere? When it comes to seaside communities where cats patrol the coastline, watching for birds and scouting for treats, Japan's famed cat islands are not alone. Ceyda Torun's wonderful 2016 documentary *Kedi* (the Turkish word for "cat") explores the complex web of human-feline interaction in Istanbul, where café owners, shopkeepers, fishermen, and veterinarians all take part in an informal cat support system. The cats, in turn, seem to keep rodents at bay, and charm locals and tourists as only cats can. Any city that has a temperate climate, access to abandoned or unguarded snacks, sunny rooftops, and fresh fish is bound to become a Catland sooner or later.

A cat named Chako sits on a pedestal with a sign reading: SOLELY FOR CHAKO, beside a temporary housing unit in Minamisanriku, Miyagi Prefecture, for people hit by the March 2011 earthquake and tsunami (photo taken February 2, 2012).

Adoptable residents at the Black Cat Café in Himeji in 2014.

But lovely as it sounds, I didn't grow up with a Turkish cat character on my elementary school pencil case, and chances are, neither did you. The reason that those of us who live outside of Japan are apt to see it through a cat-shaped lens is because we encounter Japanese cat imagery starting in childhood. Japan gave the world Hello Kitty, Doraemon, YouTube star Maru, and the Cat Bus, a character from Hayao Miyazaki's film *My Neighbor Totoro*, among others. The Cat Bus is exactly what it sounds like: a grinning orange tabby whose body is fitted with cozy, fur-covered seats. Hello Kitty alone is the second highest-grossing franchise ever, with $80 billion in sales since she premiered in 1975.

Keio Tama-Center Stationmaster Manabu Shimokawa and Hello Kitty during her one-day stint as a stationmaster in Tokyo in 2014, celebrating her 40th anniversary.

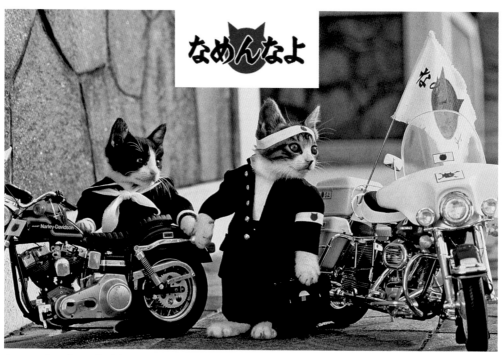

Inside Japan, it's even better. TV commercials for the travel company Jalan have featured a pair of kimono-clad cats that travel the country together with tiny suitcases, and a bespectacled cat sporting a necktie who presents a fish-shaped business card to colleagues while on a work trip. In another commercial, a larger-than-life cat appears out of nowhere on a subway platform when a commuter starts chewing Fit's Link gum, proceeding to carry the man to work through Tokyo's morning rush hour. On the train, the man lies on the cat's back and makes snow angels in its dense fur, delighted. Tellingly, a Google search for "cat businessman commercial Japan" yields multiple excellent results.

なめんなよ

An image from Satoru Tsuda's *Nameneko* series, which depicted kittens as juvenile delinquents, ca. 1981.

40分

All of these famous Japanese cat personae (with the exception of Maru) have one thing in common: none of them are pets. According to a 2016 worldwide survey by the German consumer research firm GfK ("Growth from Knowledge") SE, the top cat country in the world by total cat population is actually the United States, with a total of 74,059,000 pet cats, and a human population of about 327 million. Japan has 9,649,000 pet cats and a human population of nearly 127 million. Per capita, about one in 13 households in Japan have at least one cat, while one in 4.5 American households do. One reason for this is that it can be challenging to have pets in Japan. Many apartment buildings have restrictions on animals, and landlords are apt to allow one small dog but forbid cats altogether—the opposite of typical pet rules in the United States.

A sign for the Wan Nyan Chu Cat Café in Tokyo.

Apprentice Stationmaster Tontama (left) and Stationmaster Nitama (right) with Mitsunobu Kojima, president of Wakayama Electric Railway Co., at a ceremony in 2017.

Mitsunobu Kojima holding Kishi Stationmaster Nitama at the opening ceremony of the Tama Jinja shrine next to the Wakayama Electric Railway's Kishi Station in 2015. It's estimated that 3,000 people attended Tama's funeral. In 2014, Kishigawa Line drew as many as 2.27 million riders thanks to Tama's popularity.

These restrictions, combined with relatively small apartment sizes, put the enduring appeal of the local cat café into perspective. Cat life in Japan is widely enjoyed as a social, cultural, and even municipal phenomenon, as in the case of Tama, the calico master of Kishi Station on Wakayama Prefecture's Kishigawa rail line. (Tama passed away in 2015, but the station found an able successor in Nitama, or "Second Tama.") It isn't just that Japan loves cats; they have a shared cat *culture*. And thanks to the worldwide availability of Japanese cartoons, video games, stationery, and cat videos, we do too.

A resident bathes at Jalala Cat Café in Tokyo.

Tsuguharu Foujita (1886–1968),
Self-Portrait with Cat, color
woodcut, Japanese Shôwa era,
ca. 1928. John Ware Willard Fund,
Museum of Fine Arts, Boston.

Every cat has a touch of aristocratic hauteur, regardless of whether they were lovingly cared for from kittenhood or had to scrape by on their wits. Cats have what the English call "an eye for the main chance": they know a good thing when they see it and will tend to pad daintily toward it. Cats are sometimes described by admirers and detractors alike as "aloof," a quality that only serves to make it especially endearing when they decide to curl up next to you and purr the night away. There's something magical and complicated about living with a cat. Their wide eyes, small faces, and soft fur make them seem vulnerable and in need of care—and indeed, they often are—but their stealthy hunting prowess and acrobatic skills give them an air of wild mastery. They're cuddly, furry playmates and cold-blooded assassins, all in one. Complex, just like us.

One artist who captured the complexity of life with cats particularly well was Tsuguharu Foujita (1886–1968), also known as Léonard Tsuguharu Foujita. Born in Tokyo, Foujita became part of the Paris art world starting in the 1910s, where he was acquainted with the likes of Henri Matisse and Pablo Picasso. He was admired for his ability to combine Japanese and Western-style printmaking and painting techniques, creating portraits that seem to exist comfortably within both traditions. He also loved cats: they appear as supporting characters in many of his portraits of people, and on their own as one of his favorite subjects. His Book of Cats, a collection of 20 prints, was published by Covici Friede in 1930. His circa-1928 Self-Portrait with Cat, in which he appears wearing a blue shirt and his trademark round eyeglasses, captures his affection for a friendly tabby who's shown perched just over his left shoulder. Foujita's bemused expression paired with the determined gaze of the cat depicted in the pursuit of human attention captures something eternal about the human-feline dynamic.

In this 1950 photograph, artists Jean Cocteau and Tsuguharu Foujita celebrate with Tsuguharu's cat Karoun, crowned "King of the Cats" at an international cat show sponsored by the "Cat Friends" Club of Paris.

A relaxed cat at the Umenomiya Taisha Shrine in Kyoto.

The earliest known pet cats lived in ancient Mesopotamia, where they probably domesticated themselves about 10,000 years ago. In a 2004 interview with *National Geographic* magazine, Dr. Melinda Zeder, Curator Emeritus of Old World Archaeology and Archaeozoology at the Smithsonian Institution, described these early cats as "commensal domesticates," which is the term used for animals that are attracted to human settlement, but not deliberately sought out and raised by humans. The ancient Egyptian goddess Bastet, who has the head of a cat, was depicted early on (in the third millennium BC) with the head of a lioness. Over the course of two thousand years, Bastet's head began to appear more and more like that of a domestic cat. Ancient Egyptians increasingly perceived the cat-headed Bastet and goddess Sekhmet, who has the head of a lioness, as two aspects of the same deity: one gentle and tender, the other fierce and powerful. Royal and noble cats were loved and pampered in life, then revered and mummified in death. Not bad for a "commensal domesticate."

No human who lives with a cat would be surprised to hear any of this. Sometimes cats react to being annoyed by lashing out with a swipe of the paw. When denied something they want, they might offer a plaintive meow. But they're just as apt to respond with a kind of baffled astonishment that they—of all individuals—would be inconvenienced, perhaps assuming that the human in question cannot possibly realize whom they're inconveniencing. Their natural haughtiness, combined with their lusty passion for food, sunbeams, and soft bedding; their uncanny sense of balance; their superior hearing; and their physical elegance all combine to make them seem at once otherworldly and deeply familiar. Even as they appear to defy the laws of physics by landing on their feet time and again, they're easily distracted by the swoosh of a feather toy, or by the sounds of a snack being prepared from several rooms away. As supernatural beings go, they're unusually relatable.

The world of Japanese cat culture is vast. Enter, and you'll discover Shinto and Buddhist beliefs about animals and nature, folklore about cats both real and supernatural, cats depicted in Japanese works of art and literature over the course of centuries, cat-inspired material culture and everyday objects, cat animation, the global export of cuteness, cat tourism, and *nekonomics*—the local term for the economic boon that results from a popular cat attraction. Japan's cat culture contains multitudes, and it transcends physical geography. You might be allergic to cats. You might not be a cat person (yet). But once you've been beckoned inside, the chances are good that you'll decide to stay a while.

Welcome to Catland.

Michiko Tsuji at her sweets shop, Funahashi-ya Sohonten, in Kyoto, with one of her friendly shop cats.

JAPAN'S LUCKY CATS

日本のラッキーキャッツ

Japan's cat story is unique, but in several ways, it echoes the broader themes of humans learning to live with feline companions all over the world. There are legends invested with the gravitas of religion in which cats are noble guardians; tales and imagery of demonic, cat-like creatures terrorizing humans; and a story from medieval Japanese literature in which a frolicking kitten inadvertently sets in motion a chain of events that leads to disaster. All in a day's work.

A collection of antique ceramic maneki neko figurines.

There's relatively little documented evidence that explains how cats arrived in Japan, but it's generally believed that they first appeared in the 6th or 7th century on ships sailing from China. A popular version of this story holds that a mission from the Tang dynasty bringing Buddhist scripture to Japan also brought cats, who ably kept vermin away from the scrolls. It's entirely possible that these seafaring cats were simply curious stowaways who made the best of things once they reached Japanese soil, but that this legend exists at all says something about how cats are perceived. They may be predatory, but in the right context, they're the fierce protectors of something deeply precious and good.

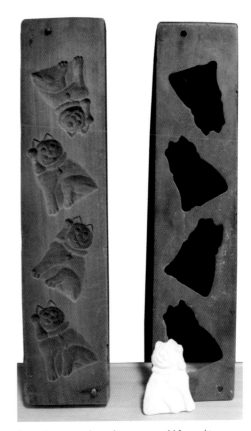

An antique carved wooden press-mold for making ceramic cat figurines from a private collection in Japan.

41

According to Dr. Sarah E. Thompson, curator of Japanese art at the Museum of Fine Arts, Boston, it's unclear precisely how cats got to Japan, but once there, they attained high status pretty quickly. She notes that a pet cat appears in *The Pillow Book*, a wonderful and witty account of life among the Japanese nobility during the Heian period, written between AD 990 and 1000 by the accomplished poet and court lady Sei Shōnagon. "Cats were highly prized at the time because they had only been in Japan for a few centuries at that point," says Thompson. "It's unclear exactly when or how they emigrated from the continent, but they may have been diplomatic gifts or expensive trade goods."

Playing with a Cat from the series *One Hundred View of Alluring Women*, color lithograph postcard, ca. 1910s–30s, Japan. Leonard A. Lauder Collection of Japanese Postcards, Museum of Fine Arts, Boston.

Quiet Cats from Ehagaki sekai, color lithograph postcard published by Kokkei Shinbun Sha, 1908, Japan. Leonard A. Lauder Collection of Japanese Postcards, Museum of Fine Arts, Boston.

Among the earliest evidence for pet cats in Japan is the diary of Emperor Uda (AD 866–931), who wrote an entire entry called "For the Love of a Cat" in the spring of 889. Written over a thousand years ago, the emperor's description is alive with delightful details that will ring true to contemporary cat lovers:

> My cat is a foot and a half in length and about six inches in height. When he curls up, he is very small, looking like a black millet berry, but when he stretches out, he is long, resembling a drawn bow. The pupils of his eyes sparkle, dazzlingly bright like shiny needles flashing with light, while the points of his ears stick straight up, unwaveringly, looking like the bowl of a spoon. When he crouches, he becomes a ball without feet, resembling a round jade taken from the depths of a cave. My cat moves silently, making not a single sound, like a black dragon above the clouds. By nature, he has a preference for Taoist-style health practices and instinctively follows the "five-bird regimen."

Ōide Tōkō (1841–1905), *Cat Watching a Spider*, album leaf; ink and color on silk, ca. 1888–92. Charles Stewart Smith Collection, Metropolitan Museum of Art, New York City.

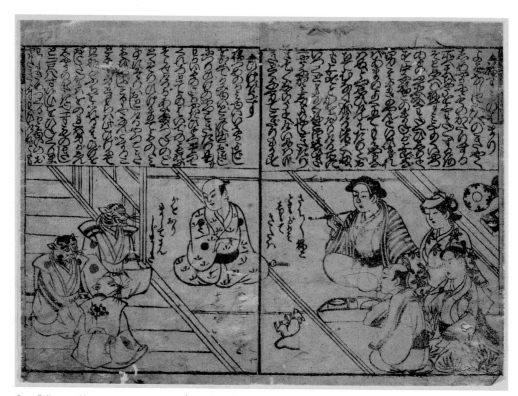

Cats Talking to Humans, woodblock print (sumizuri-e) from an unidentified Edo period book, ca. 1680s–90s. William Sturgis Bigelow Collection, Museum of Fine Arts, Boston.

He later surmises the lustrous quality of his cat's fur might be due to his Taoist-style health regimen. Emperor Uda inherited the cat from his predecessor, who in turn received it as a gift from a Japanese government official serving abroad in China, but it's instantly clear from his besotted description that he was a dyed-in-the-wool cat person, and that his pet was a cherished member of his household. (Indeed, most cats today would probably not turn their noses up at a "five-bird regimen.")

Writing in the catalog essay for her exhibition, *The Life of Cats: Selections from the Hiraki Ukiyo-e Collection*, at New York's Japan Society in 2015, Dr. Miwako Tezuka notes that while cats quickly assumed a comfortable perch among Japan's upper classes, they also developed a complex reputation.

A devilish kitten triggers an important plot twist in one of Japan's most famous works of literature, *The Tale of Genji*, written in the 11th century by a lady-in-waiting at the imperial court, under the pseudonym o f Murasaki Shikibu. In the story, the character of Third Princess is relaxing in her quarters (and not dressed for company) when her energetic kitten happens to knock over a screen, thus revealing her to a group of young men outside. The group includes the protagonist Hikaru Genji's nephew, Kashiwagi, who falls in love with her. Kashiwagi and Third Princess have a son out of wedlock named Kaoru Genji, who becomes the antihero of the story, which involves a complex tangle of court intrigue, infidelity, and tragedy.

A feline resident sits hidden at Umenomiya Taisha, a shrine near Kyoto.

二品親王女三宮

Yōshū (Hashimoto) Chikanobu
(1838–1912), *The Third Princess
and Kashiwagi, from Chapter
34, New Herbs I (Wakana I)*,
from *The Tale of Genji*, triptych
of polychrome woodblock prints;
ink and color on paper, 1890. Gift
of Lincoln Kirstein, Metropolitan
Museum of Art, New York City.

***The* Chōjū-jinbutsu-giga** (also known as the *Chōjū-giga*, or "animal caricatures") is one of the most famous "picture scrolls" in Japan. Created over a period of decades during the 12th and 13th centuries for Kyoto's Kōzan-ji Temple, the *Chōjū-giga* comprises a series of funny anthropomorphic drawings of monkeys, rabbits, frogs, and toads, seen bathing, attending religious ceremonies, wrestling, thieving, and praying. It's likely that they were created by a monk who used animal stand-ins to satirize self-important priests. There's only one cat in the *Chōjū-giga*, and according to Sarah E. Thompson: "He's kind of a bad guy—at least, the two mice in the same scene are clearly afraid of him. They are all in a crowd of animals watching a dance by frogs. But the scene does remind us that although cats may be cute, they are also fierce little predators who terrorize their prey."

There is a belief in Shintoism, Japan's oldest religion, that every facet of the natural world, from animals and plants to rivers and mountains, is animated with a spirit known as *kami*. To the extent that *kami* are made manifest in animals, cats are certainly part of that spiritual continuum. But they have a more complicated relationship to Buddhism. Miwako Tezuka notes that there's one legend in particular that could suggest a critique of cats' character.

> There is a category of religious paintings called *nehan-zu* [nirvana painting] that depicts the moment of the Buddha's death. The legend says that all his disciples and the sentient beings gathered around his deathbed to send him off to the state of nirvana—from mice and snakes to dogs and monkeys (all 12 zodiac animals), and more—you name it. Who was missing from the scene? Cats! Cat-lovers would laugh and nod in understanding, I think.

Whether this was an intentional gesture of satire on the part of the creators of these nehan-zu scenes or a total coincidence, it certainly sounds plausible that the cats in question simply overslept.

The German doctor and naturalist Engelbert Kaempfer (1651–1716) visited Japan in the early 1690s. For two years, he studied the local flora and fauna and recorded his impressions of daily life in a book called *History of Japan*, which was published posthumously in 1727 (it can still be found today as *Kaempfer's Japan: Tokugawa Culture Observed*.) The cats he observed sound a lot like Japanese Bobtails, a breed that has flourished in Japan for centuries. "There is only one breed of cat that is kept," he wrote. "It has large patches of yellow, black, and white fur; its short tail looks like it has been bent and broken." But to Kaempfer, these cats didn't appear particularly sneaky or predatory, quite the contrary: "[The cat] has no mind to hunt for rats and mice, but just wants to be carried and stroked by women."

A detail from the *Chōjū-jinbutsu-giga* ("Animal-Person Caricatures") featuring a cat, ink on paper scroll, 12th–13th centuries. Image courtesy of the Kōzan-ji Temple and the Kyoto National Museum.

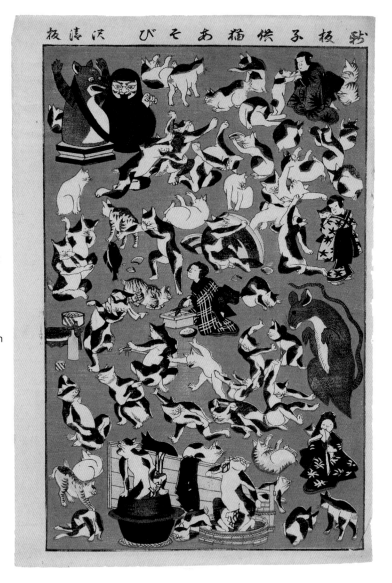

Children and Cats at Play, Newly Published, woodblock print (nishiki-e); ink and color on paper, published by Sawamuraya Seikichi, Meiji era (1868–1912). William Sturgis Bigelow Collection, Museum of Fine Arts, Boston.

Popular ukiyo-e, or woodblock prints, from the Edo period (1603–1868) feature spectacular monster cats like the *nekomata*, cats who have grown very old and transformed into terrifying creatures with split tails and the ability to speak to humans. According to Miwako Tezuka, one such creature is the antagonist of the 1827 Kabuki play *The Scene of Okazaki from the Fifty-Three Stations*. The play was so popular that it was celebrated in triptych ukiyo-e and was performed over and over to wide acclaim. But monster cats are the minority in ukiyo-e. In prints as in life, cats are more likely to appear contemplative, relaxed, playful, and funny. Cats also stand in for humans frequently in Edo-era prints.

Utagawa Kuniyoshi (1797–1861),
*Puns Just Like This: The Fifty-Three
Cats of the Ailurophile*, woodblock
print (nishiki-e); ink and color on
paper, published by Ibaya Senzaburô
(Dansendô), 1847–52.

The Edo period was a golden age for Japan's newly wealthy merchant class, who were largely excluded from hereditary seats of power, but nevertheless had the means to enjoy a life of theater, food and drink, music, and art in the newly designated Yoshiwara, or pleasure districts. *Ukiyo* means "floating world," and the *ukiyo-e* prints that documented the Yoshiwara gave art lovers access to affordable, idealized images of the fashion, humor, and beauty of their era. During this time, cats sometimes appeared—hilariously—as stand-ins for humans, fully dressed, and taking part in social rituals. They also appeared frequently alongside people in sweet, cuddly, or mischievous scenes. The artist Utagawa Kuniyoshi (1798–1861) was especially renowned for his cat ukiyo-e and *giga* (caricature) prints.

Collection of Scenes: Animals in Kabuki Roles, woodblock print (nishiki-e); ink and color on paper, 1858. William Sturgis Bigelow Collection, Museum of Fine Arts, Boston.

Utagawa Hiroshige, *The Cat of the Acrobat Crossing the Stakes Made by Dried Bonito*, ca. 1830–44. Image courtesy of the Hiraki Ukiyo-e Foundation, Tokyo.

Utagawa Kuniyoshi (1797–1861), *The Origin Story of the Cat Stone at Okabe, Representing One of the Fifty-Three Stations of the Tōkaidō Road: Actors Sawamura Sojūrō V as Teranishi Kanshin, Onoe Kikugorō III as the Spirit of the Cat Stone, and Ichimura Uzaemon XII as Ôe Inabanosuke*, woodblock print (nishiki-e); ink and color on paper, 1847. William Sturgis Bigelow Collection, Museum of Fine Arts, Boston.

Throughout the 19th century, scenes of cats visiting hot springs, trying on clothes, or taking in the sights at an industrial exhibition were popular among children, too. Artist Utagawa Kunitoshi's 1881 print *Popular Hotspring Spa for Cats* is a treasure trove that yields delight after visual delight: Look closely at the bottom of the print, and you'll find a cat food vendor tempting spa visitors with crabs on sticks as the other cats take their sandals off at the front door. One level up, cats are seen to converse and enjoy cups of tea together. One level above that, you can see a group of cats climbing up a wooden staircase to the spa, where they enjoy a soak and use traditional wooden bath buckets to splash warm water over their heads. To their right, a pair of cats enjoy the natural hot spring. And above them all, a group of post-bath cats wearing robes enjoys a light meal. One cat even clasps chopsticks while another presents what I can only assume is a serving of tasty fish. Such intricate and light-hearted illustrations are heaven for children, who can peer at each detail closely, finding a new, tiny treat with each careful viewing.

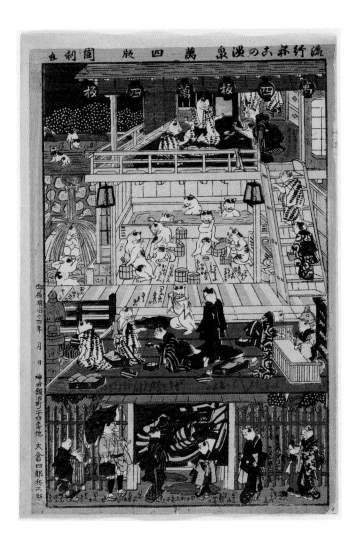

Utagawa Kunitoshi (1847–99), *Popular Hotspring Spa for Cats*, woodblock print (nishiki-e); ink and color on paper, published Ôkura Shirobei, 1881. William Sturgis Bigelow Collection, Museum of Fine Arts, Boston.

Onoguchi Tôsaburô, *Parlor in the Temporary Lodgings of the Yoshiwara Cats, Newly Published*, woodblock print (nishiki-e); ink and color on paper, 1882. William Sturgis Bigelow Collection, Museum of Fine Arts, Boston.

Utagawa Kunisada III (1848–1920),
The Cats' Industrial Exposition,
woodblock print (nishiki-e); ink
and color on paper, published by
Matsumura Jinbei, 1877. William
Sturgis Bigelow Collection, Museum
of Fine Arts, Boston.

Depictions of cats in ukiyo-e are often playful and funny, but they can also be moving and bittersweet. In *Asakusa Ricefields and Torinomachi Festival, No. 101* from *One Hundred Famous Views of Edo*, which he created near the end of his life in 1857, Utagawa Hiroshige (1797–1858), created an exquisite portrait in which the presence of a courtesan is implied, but not shown directly. A round white cat sits perched at a window, looking out over the annual celebration of the Torinomachi Festival, the one day each year in which the Yoshiwara was open to anyone. According to a description of this print in the collection of the Brooklyn Museum, this day also happened to be a *monbi*, a day in which courtesans were obligated to either take a client or pay the owner of their brothel a fee if they declined to do so.

Utagawa Hiroshige (1797–1858), *Asakusa Ricefields and Torinomachi Festival, No. 101* from the series *One Hundred Famous Views of Edo*, woodblock print (nishiki-e); ink and color on paper, published by Uoya Eikichi, 1857. William S. and John T. Spaulding Collection, Museum of Fine Arts, Boston.

Describing the piece, Dr. Susan Napier, an expert on Japanese literature and culture at Tufts University, said in an interview:

> My favorite ukiyo-e is a print by Hiroshige of a cat looking out through a lattice window from a room in the pleasure quarters. We presume that the room is occupied by a courtesan, but we don't see her, just some hair ornaments and a towel. The implication seems to be that the cat is a stand-in for the lonely/bored courtesan looking out into a wider world to which she cannot escape.

Here, the cat displays all the qualities we love: a keen and patient observer, small and round, gazing at the activity outside as window cats do all over the world, then and now. But the subtle clues of the towel and hair accessories give this image a depth of feeling that transcends the endearing cuteness and fun frivolity of the more light-hearted prints.

Hiroshige's print depicts a common experience for people who live with a cat: being ignored. Enchanted with the world outside the nearest window, cats will study the landscape for hours and behave as though they're totally alone, until a clattering from the kitchen suggests a meal might be on offer. Imagine how you'd react if such a nonchalant creature singled you out and beckoned you inside somewhere: you'd probably be surprised to find that a cat had learned to communicate by waving, but truly astonished that he had taken time out of his day to seek out a human for some special, selfless purpose.

Tsukioka Yoshitoshi (1839–92),
*I Want to Cancel My Subscription
(Woman Reading a Newspaper)*
from the series *A Collection of
Desires*; color woodcut, published
by Inoue Mohei, 1878. Philadelphia
Museum of Art.

CATLAND

In her book **Lucky Cat,** the *Japan Times* Art, Life, and Style editor Mio Yamada relates several legends of the maneki neko's origin story. The most popular one dates from the 17th century: an impoverished monk at the Gotokuji Temple in Tokyo is contemplating closing the temple altogether for lack of funds. He's about to let his cat go so that it can find a master better able to care for it, but the cat loyally decides to stay with him. That night, a thunderstorm rolled in. A traveling *daimyō* (feudal lord) named Ii Naotaka happened to pass the temple and see the cat, who, much to his surprise, was waving at him to come closer. Just as he entered the temple, a tree was struck by lightning and fell on the spot where he had just been standing. His life miraculously saved, Ii Naotaka decided to donate rice to the temple and adopt it as the shrine of his high-ranking family, thereby giving it long-lasting security.

"The funny thing is," Yamada said in an interview, "cat motifs haven't always been friendly or lucky, but I think that is part of the appeal. They have a history of being mystical, intelligent, and both loyal and mischievous." In a way, it makes perfect sense that the story of a loyal cat (and not a dog) gave shape and meaning to the Gotokuji shrine. These are, after all, the animals who *may* have decided to just sleep in as the Buddha was on his way to nirvana, who chase and terrify mice, and who knock over objects and trigger catastrophes as they play. They are not perfect, and neither are we. And when they are loyal and true, it really means something—precisely because they're not programmed to be that way: they've chosen it.

NEKONOMICS

ネコノミクス

"I am a cat. As yet, I have no name." So begins one of the great allegorical novels of turn-of-the-20th-century Japan, I Am a Cat by Natsume Sōseki (1867–1916). First published in installments as a short story in 1905, the book is a biting critique of Japanese society at the end of the Meiji era (1868–1912). The book's nameless narrator is a stray cat who gets adopted by the family of a teacher. They treat him indifferently, and he develops a pervasive disdain for humans, discussing his criticisms at length with other neighborhood cats. He tells his story with an arch disregard for the humans he lives with, and clearly sees himself as socially superior, confirming—if true—all our worst fears about how cats perceive us.

A mural at the Black Cat Shrine, Tashirojima Island Historical Museum.

Over a century later, the writer Hiro Arikawa published *The Travelling Cat Chronicles*, which opens with this sentence: "I am a cat. As yet, I have no name. There's a famous cat in our country who once made this very statement." What could be more endearing than a cat narrator with extradiegetic knowledge of a century-old novel? This detail is included with little fanfare, and it's not the premise of the book, which is more tear-jerker than satire. But it speaks to the presence of a cat culture that thrives across different mediums, from art and literature to pop culture, video games, and the web.

A relaxed resident of the Calico Cat Café in Tokyo.

There's a term for the net economic benefit that cats or cat imagery bring to a community in Japan: *nekonomics*. The term also refers to the ups and downs of the cat marketplace more broadly: sales of cat accessories and food and the financial health of cat cafés and other cat attractions. In the decades following the end of the Second World War and the American occupation, a rebuilt and broadly industrialized Japan experienced a series of economic "miracle decades." But the country had to steward its global image carefully. Instead of military might, it projected cultural, or "soft" power abroad. Post-war Japanese cinema and goods attracted viewers and shoppers from around the world. The cat icons we recognize around the world today were designed in Japan in the early '70s.

The first was Doraemon. Designed by the team of Hiroshi Fujimoto and Motoo Abiko working as Fujiko Fujio, Doraemon's manga series made its debut around 1970. Bright blue, missing his ears, and all smiles, Doraemon is a robotic cat who's sent back in time by a young boy living in the 22nd century. The boy theorizes that his family's fortunes will be better if the life of his great-great-grandfather, Nobita, improves, so Doraemon's mission is to help Nobita turn things around.

The name Doraemon loosely translates as "stray cat." Though he's smiling and cheery, his physical appearance bears the hallmarks of a rough-and-tumble street cat origin story. Originally bright yellow in color and an accomplished mouse hunter, one day his ears are bitten off by a mouse as he sleeps. When he first sees his new ear-less visage at the hospital, he's so distraught that he turns blue. Doraemon may be imperfect, but his struggles make him a sympathetic friend to the little boy he's sent to help. And in his nearly 50-year career as a manga icon, he's become one of Japan's most beloved. He has genuine cat magic about him, too: from his 4th-dimensional pocket, he can create money, food, medicine, and, best of all, desserts from the future. He was even named "anime ambassador" by Japan's foreign ministry in 2008.

While Doraemon is wildly popular in Japan, the cat icon most familiar with the west is Hello Kitty. Hello Kitty was first designed by Yuko Shimizu in 1974 and appeared on a plastic coin purse in 1975. She has been designed by Yuko Yamaguchi since 1980, and debuted in the United States in 1976. Observant Hello Kitty fans have wondered if she's based on the design of the maneki neko, which would make sense given that she appears to be a small white cat who stands upright and, presumably, says "hello," but her parent company Sanrio has never confirmed this.

In 2014, Sanrio actually revealed a twist: Hello Kitty is not a cat after all. To say that this announcement surprised fans all over the world is an understatement. That year, University of Hawaii anthropology professor Dr. Christine Yano (who literally wrote the book on the subject: *Pink Globalization: Hello Kitty's Trek Across the Pacific* from Duke University Press) was in the process of organizing an exhibition in honor of Hello Kitty's 40th anniversary. She curated *Hello! Exploring the Supercute World of Hello Kitty* at the Japanese American National Museum with Jamie Rivadeneira, who owns the boutique JapanLA.

The first coin purse featuring Hello Kitty on display at the Japanese American National Museum in Los Angeles in 2014.

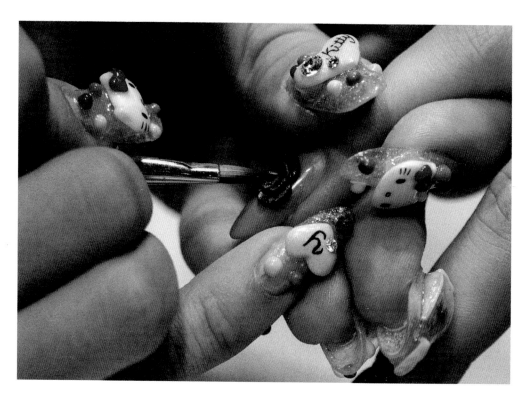

In a 2014 interview with Carolina A. Miranda of the *Los Angeles Times*, Yano said that when she sent the text she had written for the exhibition to Sanrio, their only critique was to let her know that Hello Kitty is not a cat. "She's a cartoon character. She is a little girl. She is a friend. But she is not a cat," Yano told Miranda. "She's never depicted on all fours. She walks and sits like a two-legged creature. She does have a pet cat of her own, however, and it's called Charmmy Kitty." The narrative that Hello Kitty (whose real name is Kitty White) is a British child who lives outside London was a deliberate choice on the part of her creators, who were tapping into contemporary Japanese tastes. "[I]t's interesting because Hello Kitty emerged in the 1970s when the Japanese and Japanese women were into Britain," Yano told Miranda. "They loved the idea of Britain. It represented the quintessential idealized childhood, almost like a white picket fence. So the biography was created exactly for the tastes of that time."

If Doraemon represents a factory-imperfect but loving and rather wonderful future, Hello Kitty appears to represent an idealized past that never was. In both cases, the creature in question (robot, cat, or cat-adjacent British girl) is supernatural. Cats really get supernatural in Hayao Miyazaki's 1988 masterpiece *My Neighbor Totoro*, which features a fantastical Cat Bus or *nekobasu*, the twelve-legged tabby who appears at a bus stop, his eyes glowing like headlights, to pick up protagonists Satsuki, Mei, and lovable creature Totoro. One of the most fantastical features of the Cat Bus is that he seems to be capable of transporting people anywhere they wish to go, even if they themselves don't know how to get there.

A paper lantern in the form of Cat Bus, a character from *My Neighbor Totoro*, in Minamisoma, Fukushima Prefecture, on New Year's Eve, 2012.

All of these critters would be described in Japan—and possibly in many other places around the world—as *kawaii*. Kawaii is a word in Japanese that translates roughly as "cute" in English, but it's also an entire culture with its own aesthetics. Cute mascots, symbols, and signs are everywhere in Japan, and this acceptance and enjoyment of cuteness in public life (outside the realm of early childhood, for example) is relatively unusual in other parts of the world. There's also an implicit association with cats when kawaii goes abroad. The popular adoption center and cat café near where I live in Philadelphia happens to be called the Kawaii Kitty Cafe.

A cat café in Tokyo decorated with scenes reminiscent of Utagawa Kunitoshi's 1881 print, *Popular Hotspring Spa for Cats.*

So, is kawaii culture as we know it today deeply rooted in Japanese history? Are cat-themed ukiyo-e proof that cat culture, as we understand it, is older than we thought? Not necessarily, according to Dr. Laura Miller, the Ei'ichi Shibusawa-Seigo Arai Endowed Professor of Japanese Studies and professor of history of the University of Missouri, St. Louis.

"I don't think we can look at cats in Edo period art and then say there's some connection to contemporary cat art and cat culture," she said in an interview. "That's a type of cultural essentialism that, although it is the bread and butter of Japan Societies, is not anything that scholarship supports. That's like saying 'People liked to paint about food in 1600s Europe, so that's why contemporary European art has images of food.'" What's more likely is that today's cat cultural zeitgeist has triggered a renewed enthusiasm for depictions of cats in Japanese art history, and it's natural for people to draw comparisons between past centuries and our own time—for instance, imagining that popular cat-themed ukiyo-e were akin to Edo era "cat memes." Miller notes that the global love for all things kawaii, at least in its cutest incarnation, is the result of savvy marketing starting in the 1970s. Cue Hello Kitty and Doraemon.

A security guard at the Onomichi City Museum of Art, where a pair of cats named Ken Chan and Go Chan have been trying to get in since at least 2016.

For Miwako Tezuka, who carefully considered the concept as she was organizing *The Life of Cats* exhibition at the Japan Society in New York, it's largely an aesthetic one: "I think the trend of 'kawaii' derives partly from the long-lasting Japanese aesthetic sensibility that leans toward things that are small, fragile, and impermanent (also meaning constantly changing)." Things that are kawaii are typically not just cute, but vulnerable. Brooke Hodge, director of architecture and design at Palm Springs Art Museum, thinks it might be a form of subtle international marketing:

> I almost wonder if the branding of Japanese goods as 'cute' is directed more toward foreign audiences who don't have the knowledge of history and tradition that most Japanese do, and that would lead to other readings of small and exquisite objects. I think the small size as a design virtue makes sense in a country where everything is smaller and quieter, and not as brash as we might find here [in the US] or in the UK.

きゃりこ新宿店オープン9周年記念企画

当店のオープン記念日である3月12日（月）にご来店のお客様には

きゃりこオリジナルデザイントートバッグ

こちらのキャンペーンは
終了いたしました。

プレゼント！

また、3月12日から3月22日までの期間中にご来店のお客様には

吉祥寺店・新宿店どちらでも使える
500円割引券

プレゼント！

※有効期限は2018年6月30日まで

お会計はこちら
¥CASHIER¥

An attentive cashier at the Calico Cat Café in Tokyo.

In 2009, Japan's Ministry of Foreign Affairs began appointing a group of "kawaii ambassadors," who were largely focused on fashion. "The Kawaii Ambassadors were absolutely an intentional projection of Japan's soft power," says Mio Yamada of the *Japan Times*, though she notes that the program appears to have been short-lived. Anne Ishii, the director of Philadelphia's Asian Arts Initiative and a translator who works between Japanese and English, says that kawaii is also a catch-all term in Japan, much the way "cool" is in the United States. So while it often means "cute," it can also just mean "beautiful" or "desirable."

An alert resident of the JaLaLa Cat Café in Tokyo.

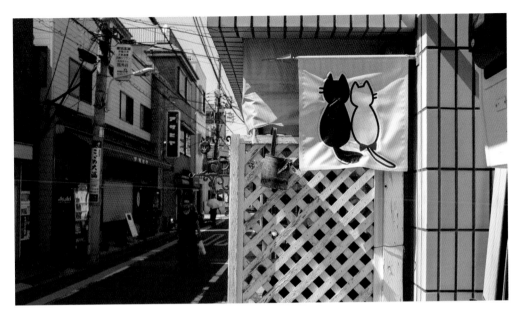

As popular as all of these characters—cute, kawaii, and otherwise—are in Japan, they're beloved in the rest of the world too, to an extent that would probably not be possible without the internet. Japanese pop culture was a global export back when Sanrio goods hit American store shelves in the mid-1970s. But since the advent of the web, cats in particular have gained global traction, and this has meant perfect conditions for cat-themed content. Anyone can watch a Japanese movie or TV show with subtitles or read a novel in translation, but there will always be a piece missing if you don't understand the language. Not so with cat culture: Japanese cat life is unique, but the love of cats is global, and it knows no language barrier.

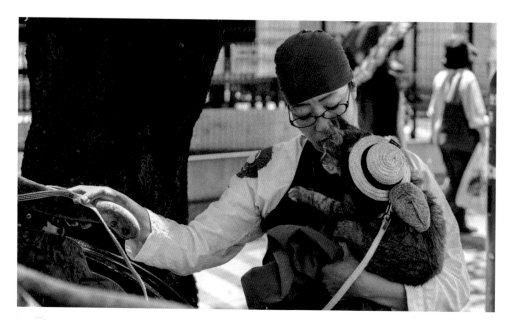

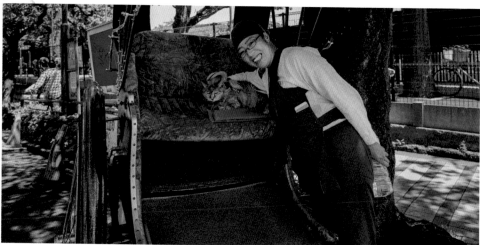

Rumi Kondoh and her cat Mii-chan. Rumi drives a rickshaw in Tokyo, occasionally bringing Mii-chan along with her.

Cats and cat attractions are now pretty easy to find throughout Japan, which has over 150 cat cafés. The very first cat café actually opened in Taipei, Taiwan, in 1998, but the concept flourished in Japan, where cafés often stock libraries of manga for visitors to read while they enjoy the cats' company. For the more adventurous, Japan's "cat islands," reachable by ferry, offer a rustic, rural place to explore and encounter semi-feral cats. Some islands—such as Tashirojima in Miyagi Prefecture, which has a cat shrine—have veterinarians regularly visit to help care for kittens and cats who need medical attention. One theory as to how Tashirojima ended up with so many cats is that the silk industry made use of cats to keep rodents away from silkworms during the Edo period. The silk industry moved away, but the cats remained.

Cat shrines in Japan don't just have figurines; some of them have communities of cats who are cared for by monks and neighbors. The Umenomiya Shrine in Kyoto, which was established in the year 965, has been keeping cats since 2000 and has become a local attraction for photographers and cat-lovers alike. Gotanjo-ji Temple in Echizen in Fukui Prefecture was founded in 2002 and began keeping cats right away. Established to honor a 13th-century Zen master who was born in the region, the temple sheltered a group of four abandoned cats in a cardboard box, and today they care for about 30 cats, according to Chief Priest Akiyori Inawashito, who notes that they spay and neuter the cats to prevent overpopulation, and each cat is available for adoption. "30,000 cat lovers from all over the country come here every year to be healed by cats," he says. "This temple is a new temple, not a national treasure, or something famous. We didn't have anything. But cats have become our guide, and now it is a [good] temple for matchmaking."

Emiko Hashimoto and friendly cats at the Umenomiya Shrine near Kyoto.

Visitors to Tokyo's Imado Shrine like to catch a glimpse of Nami, a white stray cat who lives there. She's believed to bring good luck.

Mochihiro Hashimoto and a feline pal at the Umenomiya Shrine near Kyoto.

Nyannyan-ji Temple in Kyoto takes the form of a shrine, but it's equal parts art gallery and cultural attraction. Nyannyan-ji opened in November 2016, when the artistically-inclined and cat-loving Kaya family decided to create a new kind of cat temple. Painter Toru Kaya and his son, Miyano, who also enjoys painting cats at home, have their art studio there, and his wife, Junko Kaya, crafts needle-felted animals and toys for the temple's shop and offers instruction in the classroom almost every day. There are two cafés on-site as well, but the undisputed stars of Nyannyan-ji are the temple cats, who are sweetly dressed in temple garb. Toru Kaya notes that it's not truly a shrine in the same way as Umenomiya or Gotanjo-ji, but rather "a temple-type theme park with a cat as its main prize." Real monks do visit, however, and the cats—including fluffy Aruji, whom Toru says is practicing to become a monk—don't seem to mind.

Cat priest Koyuki at Nyannyan-ji Temple in Kyoto.

Aruji, a cat monk in training.

Junko, Miyano, and Toru Kaya, the family of artists who run Nyannyan-ji Temple together.

Almost like Utagawa Kunitoshi's
Popular Hotspring Spa for Cats come to
life, Murasaki-yu in Kyoto is a family-run
sentō, or public bathhouse, that has a
cat on site. Nobuko Hayashi's family has
owned the bath for about 50 years, and
they live on the second floor. Years ago,
she started bringing her pet cat, Hinata,
with her to work at the spa. The bathhouse
runs just like any other (there are no cats
in the baths themselves), but Hinata has
gained nationwide attention as Murasaki-
yu's fastidiously clean, orange mascot.
When asked what makes cats so appealing,
Hayashi says that cats are cute, and not
obedient like dogs, which makes them even
more adorable, describing the ambiance
afforded by cats as "warm existence."

For travelers who truly cannot get enough cat company, the Beppu Aratama Ryokan Onsen, a traditional hot spring hotel near Ōita, is a cat mecca. Like any well-run cat attraction, Aratama has rules, but its popularity with visitors from abroad has posed some challenges, says owner Fujie Goto, whose family has run the hotel for nearly a century (it has had a cat focus for 16 years). The hotel has strict hygiene protocols designed to protect the cats' health and wellbeing. The hotel runs like a very large cat café, where the cats have numerous rooms to play and interact with visitors, who must wash their hands and wear sturdy clothing. Goto works closely with Animal Rights Center Japan, taking in abandoned cats, neutering and spaying them, and addressing any medical needs they have, then helping them find new homes whenever possible. And any cats who are not adopted are welcome to stay at the hotel forever. "Taking care of kittens in this way, when I transfer them [to a new home] I feel happy for them, and at the same time very lonely," she says. "It really feels like a mother giving away a bride."

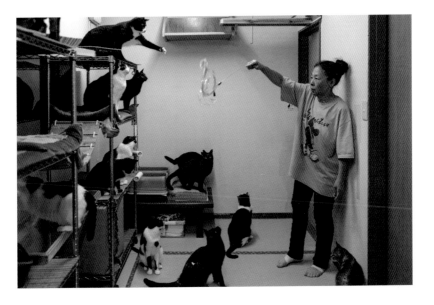

In Fukuoka City, retired curator Miyako Okubo runs a cat-themed bookshop called Wagahaido, which she started as an online shop in 2013. Today, she has visitors from all over the world and even published a book with Yosensha Press called *Neko Hon'ya Hajimemashita Tankōbon* (*I Started a Cat Bookstore*). She says that books on cat ukiyo-e and foreign cat books sell well, but her personal favorite is the classic 1936 American children's book *Mittens*, by Clare Turlay Newberry.

Jinbōchō Nyankodō in Tokyo is somewhat akin to a cat café in that you can order coffee and read a magazine while curious cats peek at you, but it's actually a cat-themed bookstore. Shop founder Fumio Anegawa donates a portion of the proceeds from the sale of books, magazines, and custom tote bags to support the city's population of street cats. As Jinbōchō Nyankodō is not a cat café, visitors are asked to admire the shop's feline residents only from afar.

Owner Fumio Anegawa holding a custom print by illustrator Tamami Kumakura at Jinbōchō Nyankodō bookstore in Tokyo.

Japan has numerous YouTube and Instagram cat stars, the most famous of all is a male Scottish Fold named Maru. Maru's name translates, delightfully, as "round," and his human goes by the moniker Mugumogu. Mugumogu has been capturing Maru's antics and posting videos to her YouTube channel since 2008. (Maru now appears with younger sister Hana, who joined the family in 2013.) Maru's face and affect are a pitch-perfect match for his medium: his round, almost Churchillian pout makes him look at once adorable and slightly annoyed, yet he tackles challenges—from flattening out to shimmy under a series of ever-lower pieces of cardboard, to jumping into shopping bags, and demonstrating his brave indifference to the scary vacuum cleaner—with aplomb. Mugumogu has upward of 720,000 subscribers on YouTube who enjoy the comic understatement of the title cards she uses to open each video. The cardboard shimmying video opens thus: "This is an experiment video to inspect 'How flat can cats become?'"

CRAFTS

工芸

The web has also made it easier for people around the world to find specialized, handcrafted goods from Japan that are made especially for, or are inspired by, cats. Japan's craft economy is robust and enjoys both governmental and popular support at home. Japanese mass-market goods and entertainment have little trouble finding eager audiences abroad, but smaller businesses and makers typically don't have the benefit of worldwide icons like Hello Kitty to capture the popular imagination. That is, they didn't until some of them realized that catering to cats as clientele could shine a spotlight on fine local craftsmanship across Japan.

Yuko Tannai (top) and Hanako Kawauchi (bottom) at work on neko chigura.

The town of Sekikawa in Japan's coastal Niigata Prefecture is home to a cottage industry of *neko chigura*, or cat baskets. One workshop there, the Sekikawa Village Cat Hut Society, has been producing these baskets since 1981. The baskets began appearing on Western design and pet blogs in the mid-2010s. Today, many workshops in the Niigata region, including the Cat Hut Society, have large waiting lists. Cat Hut Society baskets take about a week to make, and the artisans use a specialized wire tool to weave Koshihikari rice reeds into the baskets' characteristic dome shape. Their materials are grown nearby, and kittens are often on hand to test-drive the baskets. Their brochure notes that the design of these cat baskets might be a variation on old-fashioned baby baskets, which may have been adapted for cat use as far back as the Meiji era (1868–1912). Realizing that cats today are apt to make themselves at home on beds and sofas, the Cat Hut Society advises taking a wait-and-see approach with a new cat basket. "They may play in the basket but ultimately sleep in bed with the owner," they note in their brochure. "This is an excellent product for the cat that is used to hanging out in boxes in a corner."

C
A
T
L
A
N
D

142

Mari Itou with a satisfied neko chigura customer.

Fukuoka Prefecture on Japan's Kyushu island has had a thriving furniture industry for nearly 500 years and has at least 150 furniture companies today. Recently Okawa Kagu, a local trade organization for furniture makers, worked with artisans to create perfectly scaled-down versions of the furniture they make for humans, aimed at cats. Launched in 2017, the collection "Craftsman MADE" features sofas and beds that look exactly like their human-sized counterparts, down to the last detail, from the polished wood to the leather and wool upholstery. In an interview, Kento Tsumura of Okawa Kagu confirms what you probably suspect, which is that the project has garnered a lot of attention, and many orders have been placed for unsuspecting cats all over the world. And they approached the project from an intriguing angle: "At first, it was not for the purpose of making cat furniture but for branding to prove Okawa's furniture technology," Tsumura says. "[A] cat is whimsical and liberated, but very greedy for the most 'comfortable place.'" The idea was that if Okawa furniture can satisfy cat clientele, they can meet requests from anyone.

From left to right: Yoshiaki Hiromatsu, Naruhiro Nakamura, and Keiko Nakahara with the Santa Fe Sofa for cats, Hiromatsu Furniture, Inc.

146   Ahkihito Ohtsubo of Hirata Chair Manufacture with a Pisolino Sofa in progress.

Ryoji Kogi, the Executive Director of Okawa Terrazza, with some of the company's cat-scaled furniture.

Maneki neko are so ubiquitous in Japan (and elsewhere) that it's somehow hard to believe that they're made in small workshops largely by hand, but many of them are! Baigetsu Tomimoto Doll Factory, Inc. in the small city of Tokoname, Aichi Prefecture, is situated in a part of Japan that has been associated with ceramics and pottery production since at least the Heian period (794–1185). Tomimoto is family run and produces a staggering 30,000 maneki neko figurines each year. They've been producing figurines here since 1945 using local clay, and there are ten people working there at any given time. The cats are slip-cast, which involves pouring liquid clay into molds then firing them once, after which they're sprayed with a base-coat glaze that gives them an overall color. Most are white, but they come in an array of colors that represent different things, as do their paw positions. Cats with their left paws raised invite people, while the right paw invites money. White cats represent happiness, while pink cats represent love, red cats represent health, yellow cats represent marriage, blue cats represent safety, and gold cats represent money. A green cat brings good luck on exams, while a black cat guards against bad luck.

Details like the cats' eyes and whiskers are painted on by hand, and there are 200 patterns to choose from.

Takako Iwasa, the tailor known to the world as "Cat Prin" (Prin was actually the name of her late cat), rose to fame in 2008 when VICE's *The Cute Show!* profiled her. She and the VICE Books team produced a book called *Fashion Cats* in 2011, which features examples of her tailoring and an interview that explains her unique career path. Iwasa started making cat fashions in 2000 when she was recovering from an illness and spending a lot of time at home. As she told VICE in an interview, she heard a booming voice telling her to "do something this year." The result—which allowed her to work from home, right as internet commerce was taking off—was a website where she sold cat costumes. Now she gets special requests year-round. She was inspired by her mother, who had made a custom cape for her cat, Prin. She works in several styles, and has a special fondness for the aesthetics of Versailles, making cat costumes that echo the embroidered finery of France's Ancien Régime. Classically English bowties, capes, and caps in plaids and tweeds are also popular.

Google knows you want to ask why the Japanese love cats, but does it have an answer? Probably not one as good as Takako Iwasa's. When asked why cats seem to be so prominent in Japanese culture, she replied: "Cats are in close contact with human life. Cats do not depend on people, but they are also good at adapting to humans. We have a saying that 'The dog attaches himself to his master; the cat attaches herself to the house.' So the existence of cats [has been] accepted in the Japanese family and house for a long time, I think." Maneki neko figurines beckon people in as they stroll along sidewalks, and in a sense, digital and popular cat culture does something similar across the globe, by catching our attention and leading it somewhere surprising. Around the corner, we might find art and religious history, cultural knowledge, good design, the stories of people devoted to animal welfare, and the cutest municipal signage anywhere in the world. When tempted by such a wealth of fascinating things, either while traveling abroad or falling down a research rabbit hole, the best advice is probably just to go forth confidently as a cat would. Be curious, adapt, never skip a nap, hold your head high, and enjoy yourself. There will always be treats.

ACKNOWLEDGMENTS

So many wonderful humans have left their paw prints on this project. I'm grateful to my stepfather, Peter Miller, who grew up on a farm and helped me understand as a young city kid that most animals aren't pets, and that we're bound to care for all of them no matter what, and to my mother, Kathy Blaney-Miller, who inculcated my love for animal stories, and, perhaps not coincidentally, Japanese history. My husband, Manny Citron, introduced me to the delights of living with cats, and helped me understand what it means to be an animal's guardian, through all the ups and downs that come with that privilege.

I'm grateful to my agent, Leslie Stoker, of Stoker Literary, and to my editor, Ann Triestman, of The Countryman Press, both of whom championed this idea from the beginning—despite being dog people. Editorial assistant extraordinaire Isabel McCarthy, Nicholas Teodoro, and Countryman alum Aurora Bell are all eagle-eyed detail mavens and big-picture thinkers rolled into one. And Sunny Eckerle created a unique cat map of Japan that perfectly captures the mood.

I owe nine lives' worth of treats and thanks to Anne Ishii, who not only introduced me

ACKNOWLEDGMENTS

to wonderful translator Atsuko Suda, but also to Rie Yamamoto, the indefatigable producer, photographer, and genius problem-solver, without whom this book would not exist. I was lucky to work with talented Tokyo-based photographer Lee Chapman, who kindly connected me to his fellow photographer and friend Giovanni Piliarvu, each of whom added their distinctive points of view to the marvelous images throughout this book. Checking facts, dates, names, and details for this project was not an easy task, and Laura Bullard did so with thoughtfulness and careful attention throughout.

Getting permission for images is notoriously tricky, and I have many curators and librarians to thank for help navigating that process across a language barrier and many time zones. At the Metropolitan Museum of Art, I was lucky to have help from Marco Leona, Masahiko Tsukada, Julie Zeftel, and Nobuko Shibayama, who also provided precious—nearly instantaneous—translation help on multiple occasions. I'm also grateful to Satomi Kito and Satoko Sakaguchi of the Kyoto National Museum, and to Masako Matsumura of the Hiraki Ukiyo-e Foundation in Tokyo.

Many experts generously weighed in with their knowledge and insights into Japanese design, craft, art and art history, cat culture, kawaii culture, and more. I'm especially grateful to Brooke Hodge of the Palm Springs Art Museum; Professor Laura Miller of the University of Missouri, St. Louis; Professor Susan Napier of Tufts University; Miwako Tezuka, Consulting Curator at Arakawa + Gins Reversible Destiny Foundation; Sarah E. Thompson of the Museum of Fine Arts, Boston; and Mio Yamada of the *Japan Times*.

This book would not have been possible without the efforts and cooperation of people from all over Japan, who kindly answered my questions in translation with help from Rie and Giovanni and accommodated visits and photo shoots, and of the many patient cats who posed (wittingly and unwittingly) for pictures. I extend my heartfelt thanks to Kento Tsumura of Okawa Kagu; Kikue Tomimoto and her family at the Baigetsu Tomimoto Doll Factory, Inc.; Takako Iwase ("Cat Prin"); Mochihiro Hashimoto of the Umenomiya Shrine, Kyoto; the Kaya family of Nyannyan-ji, Kyoto; Miyako Okubo of Wagahaido book shop, Fukuoka; Akiyori Inawashito of the Gotanjo-ji Temple, Fukui; Fujie Goto of Aratama Ryokan; Nameneko creator Satoru Tsuda, and Masaya Tanaka of Genius, Inc.; Fumio Anegawa of Jinbōchō Nyankodō bookstore, Tokyo; Nobuko Hayashi of Murasaki-yu; Rumi Kondoh of Tokyo; Mari Itou, Hanako Kawauchi, and Yuko Tannai of Sekikawamura basket workshop in Niigata; and Michiko Tsuji of Funahashi-ya Sohonten sweets shop in Kyoto. I'm so grateful that each of you made the time to share your insights, experiences, talents, and cats.

I've wanted to write about the phenomenon of cuteness and kawaii for a long time. But it wasn't until I had pets of my own for the first time as an adult that caring for an animal changed how I see the world. Cuteness had always delighted me, but becoming attuned to the habits, likes and dislikes, health challenges, and pure joy of the creatures in my care made me understand that the lure of cuteness is deceptively complex. We're drawn in by it, then bound up with all the responsibility that comes with it. Animals remind us that the tenderness we find so endearing is also a symbol of our obligation to care for them, and the world around us. Cats are like nature's deep cover emissaries: they fit into our world well enough to coexist with us, but their episodic wildness reminds us that we live on a unique and fragile planet, and we are responsible for the creatures that need us—wild, tame, and everyone in between. For some of us, cuteness is the dart that alerts us to this. I'm glad to have been struck by it.

A C K N O W L E D G M E N T S

This book is dedicated to Mr. K, with honorable mention to young Toast, the orange kitten currently sitting on me as I type this. It's a bittersweet irony that my husband, Manny, and I had to say goodbye to Mr. K—after a very long and wonderful life—right at the moment when I was putting the finishing touches on this book. Years ago, he sat by my side when I worried that I'd never publish anything, then purred next to me as I wrote each of my books. He was my amiable officemate and understated cheerleader. He was regal, gentle, occasionally grumpy, and a natural cuddler. He probably didn't set about changing my world view on purpose, but I'm really glad he did.

With love and gratitude,

どうもありがとうございました！

Sarah Archer
Philadelphia, 2020

SELECT BIBLIOGRAPHY

Arikawa, Hiro. *The Travelling Cat Chronicles*. Translated by Philip Gabriel. New York: Berkley Publishing, 2018.

Kaempfer, Engelbert. *Kaempfer's Japan: Tokugawa Culture Observed*. Translated and edited by Beatrice M. Bodart-Bailey. Honolulu: University of Hawaii Press, 1999.

Iwasa, Takako. *Fashion Cats*. New York: Vice Books, 2011.

Kuniyoshi, Utagawa. *Cats in Ukiyo-e: Japanese Woodblock Print*. Tokyo: PIE International, 2013.

Murasaki, Shikibu. *The Tale of Genji*. Translated by Dennis Washburn. New York: W. W. Norton, 2016.

Natsume, Soseki. *I Am a Cat*. Clarendon, VT: Tuttle Publishing, 2001.

Okazaki, Manami. *Land of the Rising Cat: Japan's Feline Fascination*. New York: Prestel Publishing, 2019.

Singer, Robert T. and Masatomo Kawai, eds. *The Life of Animals in Japanese Art*. Princeton, NJ: Princeton University Press, 2019.

Tezuka, Miwako. *Life of Cats: Selections from the Hiraki Ukiyo-e Collection Exhibition Catalogue*. New York: Japan Society Inc., 2015.

Yamada, Mio. *Lucky Cat*. London: Quadrille Publishing, 2018.

Yano, Christine R. *Pink Globalization: Hello Kitty's Trek Across the Pacific*. Durham, NC: Duke University Press Books, 2013.

FOR KIDS

Ita, Sam. *Tokyo Pop-Up Book: A Comic Adventure with Neko the Cat*. Clarendon, VT: Tuttle Publishing, 2018.

Kimmel, Eric A. *Three Samurai Cats: A Story from Japan*. New York: Holiday House, 2003.

CREDITS

All art by Sarah Archer unless specified below.

INDEX